EVERYDAY LIFE IN ANCIENT INDIA

KIRSTEN HOLM

PowerKiDS
press.

New York

Published in 2012 by The Rosen Publishing Group, Inc.

29 East 21st Street, New York, NY 10010

First Edition

Editor: Joanne Randolph

Book Design: Planman Technologies

Illustrations: Planman Technologies

Library of Congress Cataloging-in-Publication Data

Holm, Kirsten C. (Kirsten Campbell)

Everyday life in ancient India / by Kirsten Campbell Holm. — 1st ed.

   p. cm. — (Jr. graphic ancient civilizations)

Includes index.

ISBN 978-1-4488-6219-1 (library binding) — ISBN 978-1-4488-6397-6 (pbk.) — ISBN 978-1-4488-6398-3 (6-pack)

1. India—Social life and customs—To 1200—Juvenile literature. 2. India—Civilization—To 1200—Juvenile literature. I. Title.

DS425.H64 2012

934—dc23

                          2011027625

Manufactured in the United States of America

CPSIA Compliance Information: Batch #PLW2102PK: For Further Information contact Rosen Publishing, New York, New York at 1-800-237-9932.

Contents

Historical Overview

Asoka (uh-SHOW-kuh) (c. 300–232 BC) was one of the greatest kings of the Mauryan Empire. He ruled from around 269–232 BC. Early in his **reign**, he fought and won many wars to make his empire larger. Asoka then became distressed by the pain and suffering caused by war, and he converted to Buddhism. He used his reign to spread the teachings of Buddha through his empire and beyond.

- During the reign of Asoka, the Mauryan Empire covered almost 2 million square miles (5,180,000 sq km). It included most of present-day India, present-day Bangladesh, Iran, and Iraq.

- The empire was divided into five provinces. Each province was governed by a prince.

- Asoka believed in religious **tolerance**, and Buddhism and Hinduism flourished during his reign.

- During this time, men could have many wives.

- Men and women belonged to certain classes, or **castes**, in which they remained for their whole lives. Children belonged to the same caste as their parents, and they would marry people who belonged to the same caste. In ancient India, there were four main castes. They were the Brahmin, Kshatriya, Vaisya, and Sudra castes. Untouchables, or outcasts, were below these four and were not considered to be part of the caste system.

EVERYDAY LIFE IN
ANCIENT INDIA

KASI, INDIA, 250 BC DURING THE REIGN OF ASOKA

IT WAS CUSTOMARY IN ANCIENT INDIA FOR WOMEN TO RISE BEFORE MEN, GET DRESSED, AND START THE DAY'S WORK. THIS WAS CERTAINLY TRUE IN THE FAMILIES OF **GARLAND** MAKERS.

LIKE MANY WOMEN IN INDIA TODAY, WOMEN IN ANCIENT INDIA WORE SARIS, A LONG RECTANGULAR PIECE OF COTTON FABRIC THAT IS WRAPPED TO FORM A SKIRT AND HEAD COVERING.

AFTER DRESSING, THE WOMEN PREPARED BREAKFAST. THEY MADE FLATBREAD FROM WHEAT, ALONG WITH LENTILS AND WHEY.

KUMUDA WILL COOK THE BREAD WHEN SHE IS MARRIED!

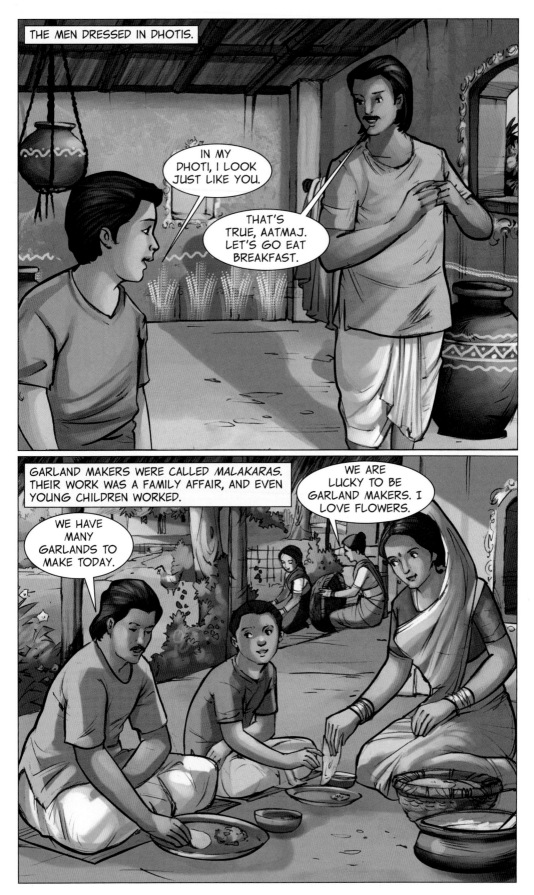

THE MEN DRESSED IN DHOTIS.

IN MY DHOTI, I LOOK JUST LIKE YOU.

THAT'S TRUE, AATMAJ. LET'S GO EAT BREAKFAST.

GARLAND MAKERS WERE CALLED *MALAKARAS*. THEIR WORK WAS A FAMILY AFFAIR, AND EVEN YOUNG CHILDREN WORKED.

WE ARE LUCKY TO BE GARLAND MAKERS. I LOVE FLOWERS.

WE HAVE MANY GARLANDS TO MAKE TODAY.

THE FAMILY HAD A GARDEN NEXT TO THEIR HOUSE. EVERY MORNING THEY CUT ENOUGH FLOWERS TO MAKE THE GARLANDS THEY SOLD.

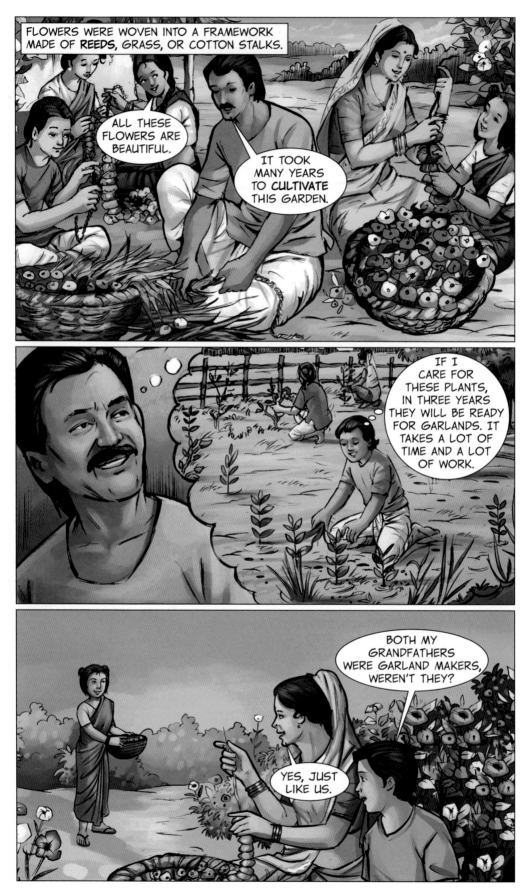

GARLAND MAKERS DID NOT JUST SELL TO THEIR REGULAR CUSTOMERS. MEN WHO NEEDED WORK BOUGHT GARLANDS, TOOK THEM TO NEARBY VILLAGES OR THE CITY, AND SOLD THEM IN THE MARKETS AND ON THE STREETS.

IN ANCIENT INDIA, GARLANDS WERE USED FOR MANY DIFFERENT TYPES OF CEREMONIES AND FESTIVALS, AND GARLAND MAKERS WERE AN IMPORTANT PART OF THE CULTURE. IN THE SIXTH CENTURY BC, MALLIKA, A GARLAND MAKER'S DAUGHTER, BECAME QUEEN.

DO YOU REMEMBER THE STORY OF MALLIKA, THE BEAUTIFUL DAUGHTER OF A GARLAND MAKER?

I'D RATHER BE A FEMALE WARRIOR AND GUARD THE KING'S **HAREM**.

I WANT TO BE THE QUEEN OF INDIA.

LIFE AT THE KING'S COURT WOULD BE BORING. I LIKE MAKING GARLANDS. I WILL BE A GOOD HELPER TO MY HUSBAND.

A PERSON'S CASTE IN THIS LIFE WAS DETERMINED BY HIS ACTIONS IN A PAST LIFE.

IN THE CASTE SYSTEM, FARMERS WERE ABOVE CRAFTSMEN BUT BELOW NOBLES AND PRIESTS. OUTCASTS HELD THE LOWEST POSITION IN SOCIETY. THEY WERE NOT PART OF THE CASTE SYSTEM.

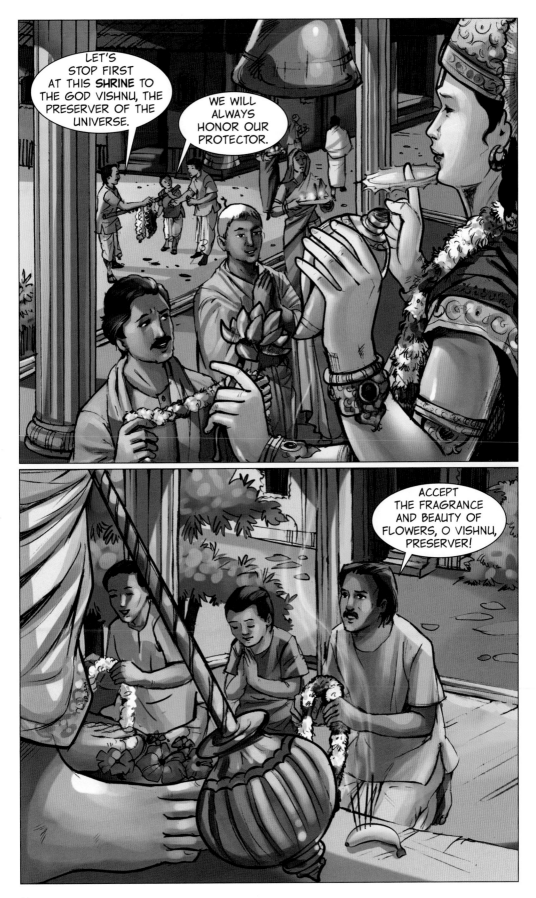

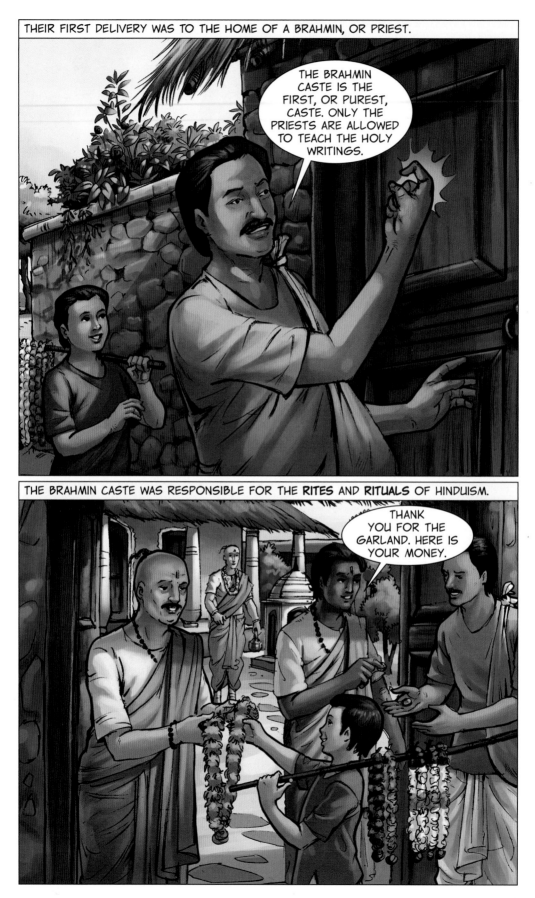

THEIR FIRST DELIVERY WAS TO THE HOME OF A BRAHMIN, OR PRIEST.

THE BRAHMIN CASTE IS THE FIRST, OR PUREST, CASTE. ONLY THE PRIESTS ARE ALLOWED TO TEACH THE HOLY WRITINGS.

THE BRAHMIN CASTE WAS RESPONSIBLE FOR THE **RITES** AND **RITUALS** OF HINDUISM.

THANK YOU FOR THE GARLAND. HERE IS YOUR MONEY.

GARLAND MAKERS, LIKE OTHER CRAFTSPEOPLE, WERE OF THE SUDRA CLASS. THE CLASS ITSELF WAS LOW, BUT GARLAND MAKING WAS MUCH RESPECTED.

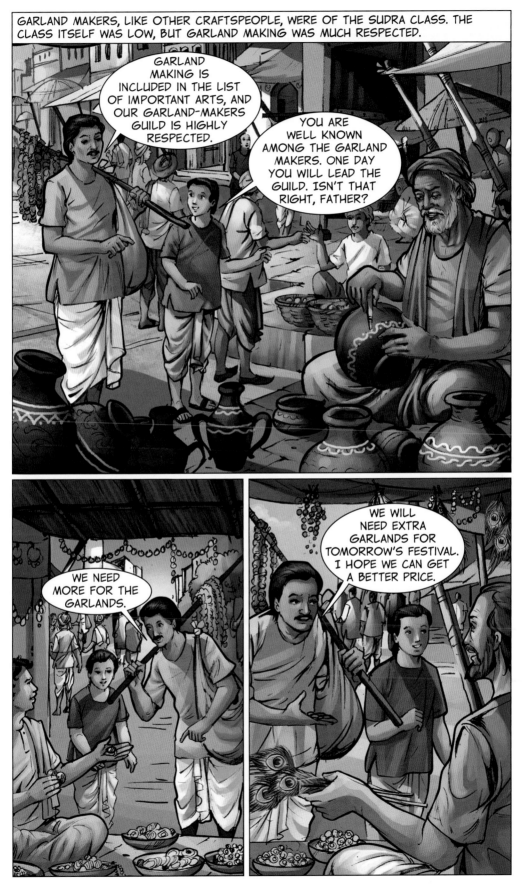

GARLAND MAKING IS INCLUDED IN THE LIST OF IMPORTANT ARTS, AND OUR GARLAND-MAKERS GUILD IS HIGHLY RESPECTED.

YOU ARE WELL KNOWN AMONG THE GARLAND MAKERS. ONE DAY YOU WILL LEAD THE GUILD. ISN'T THAT RIGHT, FATHER?

WE NEED MORE FOR THE GARLANDS.

WE WILL NEED EXTRA GARLANDS FOR TOMORROW'S FESTIVAL. I HOPE WE CAN GET A BETTER PRICE.

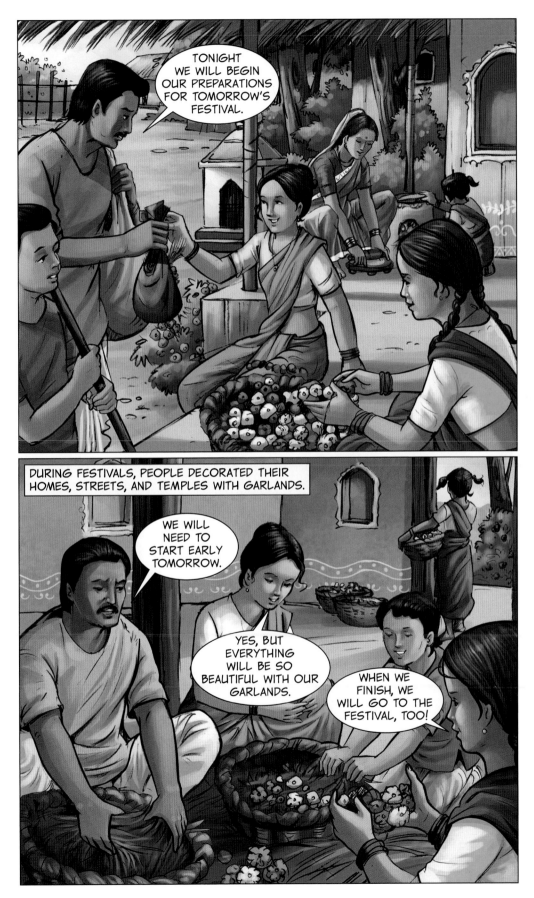

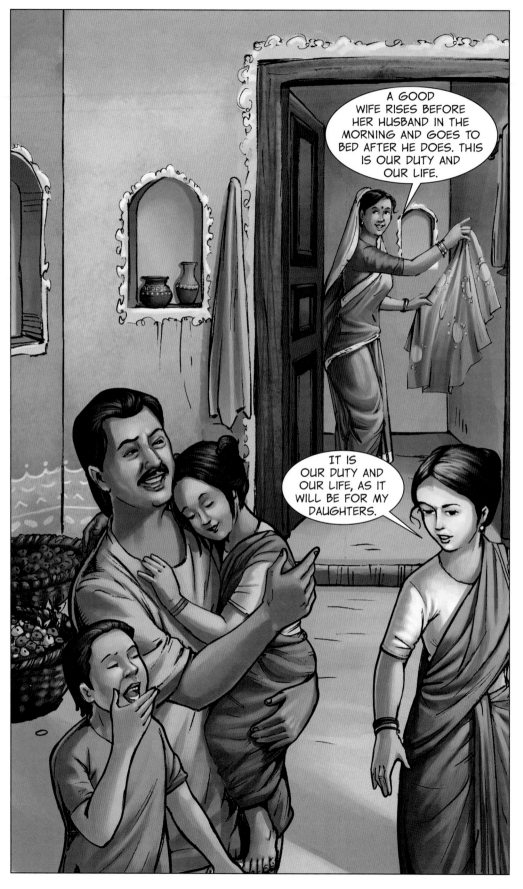

21

Did You Know?

- Ancient India is divided into four empires:

  Indus Valley Civilization (c. 2600–1900 BC) This civilization traded with ancient Mesopotamia. Although many samples of the writing have been found, no one has been able to decipher it.

  Vedic Period (c. 1800–600 BC) In this period, much of the Hindu culture, religion, and sacred writings were developed.

  Mauryan Empire (c. 322–185 BC) This period followed the invasion of India by Alexander the Great.

  Gupta Empire (c. AD 320–497) This period was the golden age of ancient India.

- In ancient India, the king's harem was often guarded by a company of female warriors. These warriors were called the flower of womanhood. Paintings show them wearing helmets and carrying spears.

- Queen Mallika, a disciple of Buddha, was the daughter of a garland maker. According to Buddhist legends, she was beautiful, clever, and kind. She became the wife of the king of Benares and Kosala.

- Sanskrit was the formal language of ancient India. The upper classes spoke and wrote in Sanskrit. Common people used other **dialects**.

- In ancient India, professional groups or guilds, called *srenis*, had political and social functions. Trade guilds set quality standards, served as banks for members, and even provided charity.

Glossary

castes (KASTS) Levels or groups of people in a society.

cultivate (KUL-tih-vayt) To grow.

dharma (DAR-muh) A person's duty assigned by divine power.

dialects (DY-uh-lekts) Kinds of languages spoken only in certain areas or by certain people.

garland (GAR-land) A circle of flowers or leaves.

guild (GILD) A group of people who do the same kind of work.

harem (HAYR-um) Part of a home where only women were allowed.

karma (KAR-muh) The force of a person's actions, which shows that every action has an effect.

reeds (REEDZ) Tall, slender grasses.

reign (RAYN) The period of time that a ruler has ruled.

rites (RYTZ) Acts done for a special purpose, often having to do with faith.

rituals (RIH-choo-ulz) Special series of actions done for reasons of faith.

shrine (SHRYN) A special place at which prayers or memorials can be made.

tolerance (TAH-ler-ens) Acceptance of other people's differences.

Index

Web Sites

Due to the changing nature of Internet links, PowerKids Press has developed an online list of Web sites related to the subject of this book. This site is updated regularly. Please use this link to access the list:

www.powerkidslinks.com/civi/india/

D0745665